...where yo[...]railroading is like up c[...]da Northern Railway Co[...]ndmark.

"Among all of t[...]a," notes William L. Withuhn, Curator, History of Technology and Transportation, Smithsonian Institution, "the Nevada Northern Railway complex at East Ely is – no question in my view – the most complete, most authentic, and best cared for, bar none. It's a living American treasure and a stand-out one."

For 100 years steam [...] continues today. You can explore what railroading w[...]sion trains, to the behind the scenes tours of the e[...]ience cinders crunching under foot as you tour the[...]takes to keep the steam locomotives going; using the same tools and techniques that have been used here for a century.

When we say up close and personal, we mean it. Work as a railroader during our week long RailCamps. Experience what it is like to be the engineer of a 100-ton steam locomotive through our locomotive rental program. Or take a cab ride and watch the crew get another train over the hill. Ride the steam powered excursion trains and listen to the bark of the exhaust from the locomotive, smell the coal smoke and get cinders in your hair.

There's just one place where you can experience real steam railroading, the original locomotives, the original buildings and depot. It's located in rural Nevada, four hours from Las Vegas, but a century back in time.

# The Ultimate Experience!

### Steam or Diesel Locomotive Rentals

### Rail Camp for Teens and Adults

### Cab Rides

### Winter Photo Shoots

Visit our Web site or call for complete details!

# NEVADA NORTHERN RAILWAY

1100 AVENUE A • PO BOX 150040 • ELY, NEVADA 89315

(775) 289-2085 • www.nnry.com • (866) 407-8326

# DAY OUT WITH THOMAS™

# All Aboard for Thomas & Friends™

**Classic Storybook Engine Chugs Into A Station Near You!**

•

**25-Minute Ride With Thomas**

•

**Meet Sir Topham Hatt**

•

**Enjoy Storytelling, Live Music & Much More!**

**www.thomasandfriends.com**

For tickets and information, visit
www.ticketweb.com or call 866.468.7630

Advance purchase is recommended.
Ticket sales are final. Events are rain or shine.

7/29

Durango & Silverton Railroad

Experience over
# 30 EXCITING TOURIST TRAINS WITH
# VACADNS BY RAIL <sup>SM</sup>

## Top 5 Escorted Tourist Train Vacations

The Royal Gorge Route

- ▶ Trains Across Colorado – 8 Day Tour
- ▶ New England Rails and Sails – 9 Day Tour
- ▶ Historic Trains of the Southwest – 8 Day Tour
- ▶ Trains and Canyons of the West – 6 Day Tour
- ▶ Historic Trains of California – 7 Day Tour

**Browse** Vacations by Rail's<sup>SM</sup> selection of rail vacations online at www.vacationsbyrail.com.

Mention *Tourist Trains Guidebook* and receive up to
## $50.00 off per person on your rail vacation!

VACATIONS BY RAIL™

The trusted authority on rail vacations in the United States, Canada, Europe & Beyond.

www.vacationsbyrail.com • 1-877-929-7245 (toll-free)

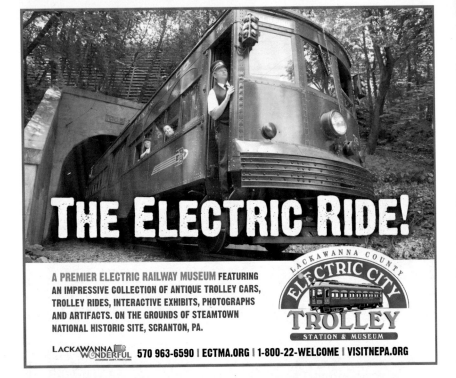
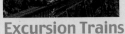

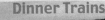

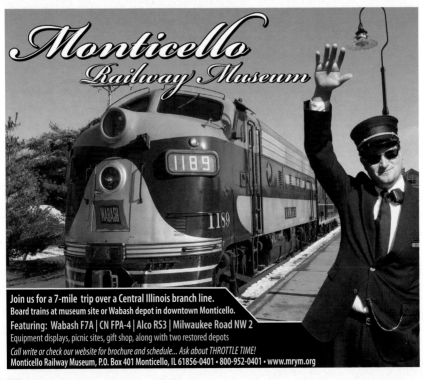

# *Enjoy*
## *a scenic Train Ride*

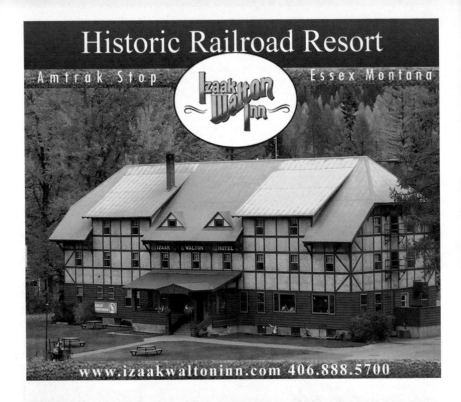

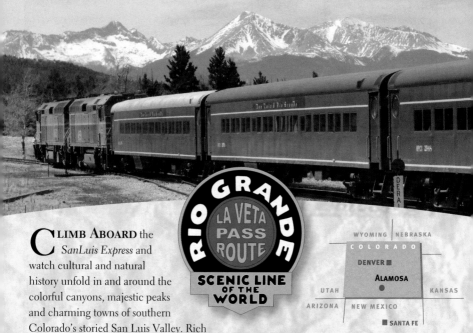

# Visit *Canada*
# Explore it *by train*

Winter, spring, summer or fall, touring by train is truly the ideal way to explore Canada, coast to coast, in comfort and style.

Whether you choose our classic train journey aboard the *Canadian*® (between Vancouver-Jasper and Toronto), our frequent intercity trains in the Québec City–Windsor corridor or the *Ocean*™, our Eastern Transcontinental (between Montréal-Moncton and Halifax), VIA Rail Canada makes travel a pleasure.

During the summer months experience daylight rail touring at its best. In Western Canada, the *Skeena*™ is your picture window on the mountain vistas of Alberta and Northern British Columbia.

Come aboard VIA and see Canada as only the train can show you!

For more information, contact your travel agent, call VIA Rail Canada at 1 888 VIA-RAIL (1 888 842-7245)
☎ TTY 1 800 268-9503 (hearing impaired)
or visit **viarail.ca**.

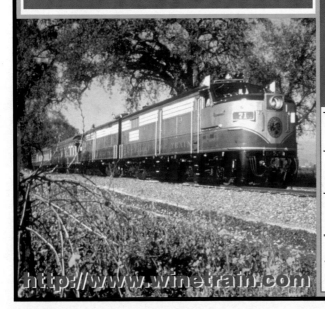
A-16

Lake Shore Railway Association operates scenic excursion rides on the Lorain & West Virginia Railway in Lorain County, Ohio from July - October

E-8 #101 & train at the Lorain County Fair
LSRA photo by M. Chappo

The L&WV offers 12 mile roundtrips at the time of publication and more trackage is being rehabilitated - Check *www.lakeshorerailway.org* for trips, schedules and fares

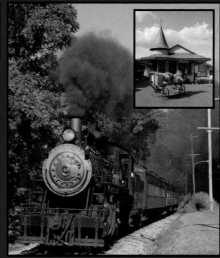

# McCLOUD RAILWAY OPEN-AIR TRAIN RIDES

*Bring the whole family for a delightful, inexpensive, excursion trip featuring either diesel locomotives or historic steam locomotive No.25. Try our new "double deck" car for incomparable views of unspoiled northern California.*

Hear the "clickety clack" as your trains winds its way around the base of Mt. Shasta. Open Air Excursion Trains depart McCloud, California. Call for schedule details.

# ALL ABOARD! SHASTA SUNSET DINNER TRAIN

*A nostalgic train ride through spectacular scenery in the shadow of Mt. Shasta featuring elegant four-course dining aboard restored vintage rail cars. A memorable evening riding the rails into yesterday!*

Experience true luxury in our 1916-vintage rail cars amid surroundings of mahogany and brass. Shasta Sunset Dinner Train departs McCloud, California, weekends year round, Thursday through Saturday June through September. Reservations are required.

To reach McCloud from I-5, take the McCloud/Reno exit and travel ten miles east turning left on Columbero Drive. Follow Columbero into town turning right after the railroad tracks.

For schedules & reservations call the

## Shasta Sunset Excursions

P.O.Box 1199 McCloud, CA 96057

## (800) 733-2141 (530) 964-2142

www.shastasunset.com
Email: info@shastasunset.com

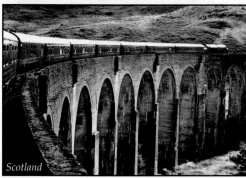

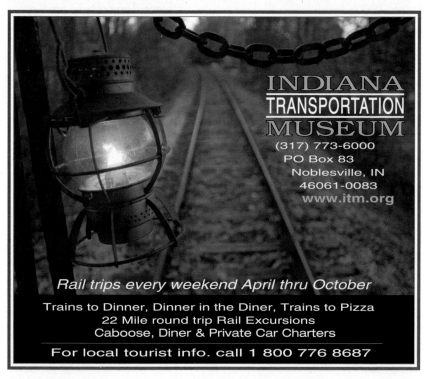

 # Stone Consulting & Design, Inc.

# RIDE THE RAILS OF THE HISTORIC BUTTE, ANACONDA AND PACIFIC RAILROAD.

Incorporated in 1892, the B.A. & P. operated between the mining and smelting communities of Butte and Anaconda, Montana. The B.A. & P. was the first railroad in the country to electrify at 2400 volts.

## The Copper King Express

The Copper King Express is a 52 mile round trip passenger excursion train over the former B.A. & P. rail line. The excursion train operates through scenic Durant Canyon and near many of the area's historic attractions:

- The World's Tallest Smokestack
- Anaconda Railroad & Mining Museum
- Beer, Wine & Soft Drinks on Train
- Guided Narration During Excursion
- Over the Historic B.A. & P. Railway
- 1953 Vintage Passenger Cars
- Historic 20 Stall Roundhouse Built in 1894

Each car has been retrofitted with video monitors that provide information on the numerous area attractions along the historic rail route. You can also enjoy a drink while riding in our refurbished 100 seat passenger cars.

The Copper King Express will depart from the new Anaconda Railroad & Mining Museum. The museum showcases the area's rich history in mining, smelting and railroading.

## RESERVATIONS ARE STRONGLY RECOMMENDED.
### All of the 2006 Regular Season Trains were Sold Out!
### Check Our Web site
# www.copperkingexpress.com
### or phone 406-563-5458
**The Copper King Express • 300 West Commerical Ave. • Anaconda, Montana 59711**

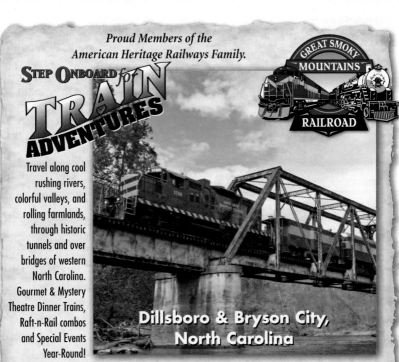

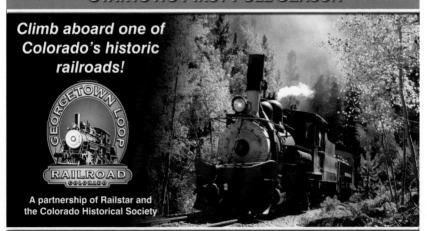

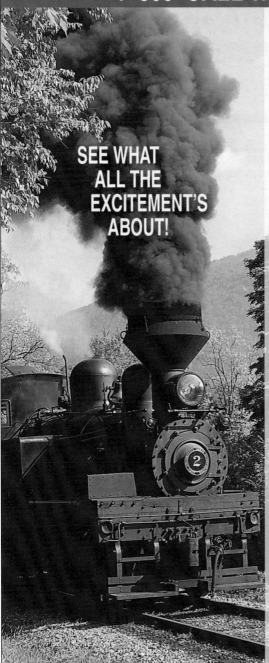
A-27

# PRIDE

## THE SOUTHERN MUSEUM

The dedicated craftsmen of the Glover Machine Works worked tirelessly to build the quality locomotives that helped rebuild the South after the Civil War.

Explore the nation's only replica of a belt-driven locomotive assembly shop and gain insight into the building process from concept through completion, including a pattern shop, factory machines, and two locomotives in various stages of completion at the Southern Museum of Civil War and Locomotive History.

Smithsonian Institution
Affiliations Program

2829 Cherokee Street • Kennesaw, GA 30144
770.427.2117 • www.southernmuseum.org

# COURAGE

## THE SOUTHERN MUSEUM

Deep into enemy territory, Yankee spies embarked on the Civil War's most daring escapade – to steal a locomotive and cut the rail supply lines to the South. The Confederate conductor saw his train leaving the station and began the Great Locomotive Chase!

Experience the thrill of the chase with an exciting movie; the stolen locomotive, the *General*; and a Medal of Honor bestowed posthumously on one of the Union soldiers after he was captured and hanged at the Southern Museum of Civil War and Locomotive History.

Smithsonian Institution
Affiliations Program

**2829 Cherokee Street • Kennesaw, GA 30144**
**770 427 2117 • www.southernmuseum.org**

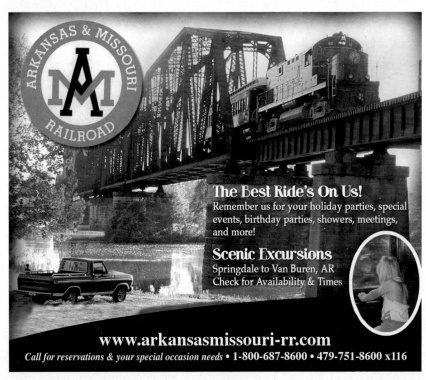